The General Care and Maintenance of
Common Kingsnakes

David Perlowin

Table of C

Introduction

Common kingsnakes, particularly the California kingsnake, are among the most popular and widely kept snakes in herpetoculture. Their beauty, moderate size, ease of maintenance, and relative docility have made them one of the most recommended snake species for the beginning hobbyist. In addition, common kingsnakes will readily breed in captivity and a wide variety of subspecies, geographical variants, and color and pattern morphs have been established by both hobbyists and commercial breeders. Relatively few snakes can match the crisp beauty and the display appeal of an outstanding desert phase California kingsnake or the variety of colors and patterns found in these North American snakes.

The purpose of this book is to provide essential information to novice snake keepers as well as serious hobbyists and professional breeders interested in keeping and breeding common kingsnakes. The information presented comes from texts and papers, conversations with kingsnake breeders, and the author's own experiences in keeping and breeding them.

The cooperation of the following people is greatly appreciated: Robert Applegate, Dorothy De Lisle, Chris Estep, Bill and Cathy Love, Paula Scarpellino, Vince Scheidt, and Gary Sipperly. Special thanks to Philippe for all his help and hard work.

1

General Information

THE NAME GAME

The scientific name for common kingsnakes is *Lampropeltis getula*. *Lampropeltis* is derived from the Greek words "lampro," meaning shiny, and "peltis," meaning shields, no doubt referring to the glossy sheen and smooth appearance of the scales.

Many of you reading this may be wondering why the species epithet is *getula* instead of *getulus*. It has been pointed out in a 1988 article in *Herpetological Review* written by Collins and Frost that technically this change needed to be made along with changing the subspecies *niger* to *nigra* and *nigritus* to *nigrita*. Usually, such changes are slow to be adopted and these are no exception. The reason given for these changes makes sense and is as follows. The word *Lampropeltis* is a feminine generic name and also requires the species name to be feminine. Thus, the name *getulus* (masculine) changes to *getula* (feminine), and the same for *L. g. niger* to *nigra*. Sometimes herpetoculturists are at odds with the so-called scientific community; often rightly so. However, in this instance everyone should be in agreement and all professional herpetoculturists and serious hobbyists should acknowledge this change. It was gratifying to observe that at the 1992 National Reptile Breeders' Expo held in Orlando, Florida, there were many kingsnake breeders who did properly name their snakes.

DISTRIBUTION

Common kingsnakes have a widespread North American distribution ranging from southern New Jersey to Florida in the east; to the west out across the central plains states and into the southwest; and from southern Oregon to northern Mexico.

ORIGIN OF PET COMMON KINGSNAKES

The most commonly offered wild-collected common kingsnakes are the Florida kingsnake, the eastern, and the speckled kingsnake. Most of the other kingsnakes now available to the public are captive-bred and sold to reptile wholesalers or directly to specialty stores. The

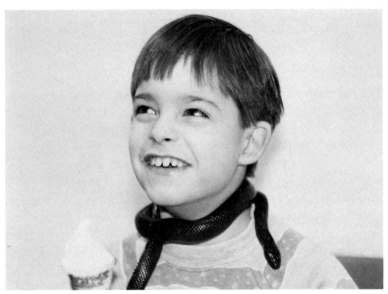

The Mexican black kingsnake *(Lampropeltis getula nigrita)* makes an excellent snake "pet" for beginning herpetoculturists. Note: as a rule snakes should not be allowed to form a complete loop around one's neck, as in this picture. Photo by Chris Estep.

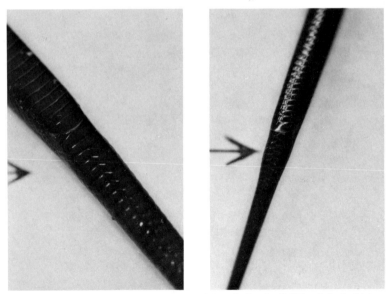

Adult kingsnakes can easily be sexed visually. The tail of males (left) is relatively thicker and tapers more gradually than that of females (right). Photo by Chris Estep.

An outstanding desert phase California kingsnake *(Lampropeltis getula californiae)*. Such specimens are highly prized by herpetoculturists. Photo by Glen Carlzen.

California kingsnake *(Lampropeltis getula californiae)*. Coastal albino banded morph. Albino California kingsnakes were among the first colubrids to be bred commercially on a large scale. Photo by Glen Carlzen.

most popular of these are the California kingsnake and its various morphs, and albino speckled kingsnakes. For those able to attend any of the reptile breeders' expos, which occur with regularity around the country, all of the subspecies (an exception is the Outer Banks kingsnake) and most of the variants of common kingsnakes are available as captive-bred babies. Many of the adult kingsnakes available are usually wild caught, although some may be either old breeders, a breeder's overstock, or captive-raised pets that owners no longer want to keep. It is a good idea to inquire about the origin of an animal before purchasing it.

HABITAT

Kingsnakes inhabit a wide range of environments. These include deserts, farm land, prairies, river banks, and deciduous forests, as well as pine forests. They can be found anywhere there is an abundance of rodents, including barns.

SIZE

Common kingsnake hatchlings range from six inches for runts to thirteen inches. Adults range from thirty six inches in speckled kings (*L. g. holbrooki*) to sixty inches in California and Florida kings (*L. g. californiae* and *floridana*), to eighty four inches in the eastern kingsnake (*L. g. getula*).

SEXING

Immature kingsnakes do not demonstrate any obvious sexual characteristics. Hatchlings and subadults are best sexed either through manual eversion of the hemipenes or with the use of sexing probes. Adult kingsnakes usually show a marked difference in the degree of taper past the vent. The tails of males, because they contain the inverted hemipenes, will appear markedly thicker at their base and not taper as sharply as the tails of females. If in doubt about the sex of a kingsnake, the use of an appropriate size sexing probe will clear this up.

PATTERN AND COLOR VARIATIONS

There will be some variation of skin color and pattern within all subspecies of common kingsnakes, but none demonstrate more distinct morphs than the California kingsnake (*Lampropeltis getula californiae*), which ranks as one of the most variable of all snakes, and the blotched kingsnake *(Lampropeltis getula "goini")*. The variations in these kingsnakes are presented in some detail in An Overview of the Common Kingsnake and in the various photographs in this book.

In terms of pattern variation in common kingsnakes, one finds in herpetoculture an emphasis on such things as width of banding, definition of pattern, or in California kingsnakes, width of striping, asymmetrical patterning or broken patterning, or reduction of pattern, as in the 90% yellow California kingsnakes, also marketed as "banana kings." In other subspecies of kingsnakes, herpetoculturists will focus on pattern definition or pattern reduction. For example, a clean, clearly defined, high contrast pattern will be emphasized by aficionados of the beautiful desert kingsnake. A reduction of dark patterning will be sought by herpetoculturists seeking to produce high quality "brooksi" morphs of the Florida kingsnake. As should be evident from the information presented so far, California kingsnakes, because of their phenotypic variability, rank among the best candidates for genetic studies on pattern and color in snakes.

The most popular and widely produced color morphs of the common kingsnake are amelanistic (lacking black pigmentation) albino California and speckled kingsnakes. In the California kingsnake, the coastal phase (brown and yellow) and desert phase (black and white) are selectively bred to emphasize these characteristics. In other kingsnake subspecies, color morphs are also being selectively bred, such as the black and orange phase of the blotched kingsnake. There are also a few anerythristic(lacking red pigmentation) south Florida kingsnakes currently in captivity which should eventually become more widespread. Additional color and pattern morphs can be expected to become available in the future because of the large-scale efforts to commercially breed common kingsnakes.

ALBINO KINGSNAKES

Several specimens of albino kingsnakes have been collected from the wild and have formed the foundation for the large numbers of albino kingsnakes now produced in captivity. Currently albinos of two sub-species, the California kingsnake and speckled kingsnake, are commercially bred on a large scale. More recently, an albino black kingsnake *(Lampropeltis getula nigra)* has been produced in captivity.

There are several genetic lines of albino California kingsnake currently established in captivity characterized by variations in eye color (i.e., ruby-eyed) and skin color (i.e., lavender). The albino trait has been introduced into most other color and pattern morphs of the California kingsnake. This has led to interesting morphs like the "albino desert phase striped California kingsnakes" and the recently developed "snow king," resulting from introducing the albino trait into the chocolate (patternless) morph of the California kingsnake. A solid lemon yellow albino is but a few years ahead. In terms of breeding, the albino trait is considered and dealt with as a simple recessive trait.

Albino (amelanistic) desert phase striped California kingsnake *(Lampropeltis getula californiae)*. This is a recessive mutation characterized by amelanism or lack of black pigmentation. Photo by Glen Carlzen.

Aberrant patterned albino California kingsnake *(Lampropeltis getula californiae)*. Herpetoculturists will use the term aberrant to describe California kingsnakes that have neither a striped or a banded pattern, but an asymmetrical or irregular one. Photo by Glen Carlzen.

A lavender/ruby-eyed albino California kingsnake *(Lampropeltis getula californiae)*. This beautiful albino morph is now well established in herpetoculture. Photo by Glen Carlzen.

HERPETOCULTURAL TRENDS

The herpetocultural trend when considering color and pattern is toward crisp, well-defined patterns and clean, contrasting colors. There is not much interest in developing genetic lines of cryptic, murky-colored kingsnakes. Thus, pure black animals are often considered more desirable than when they are black with even a suggestion of underlying pattern. Desert kingsnakes, with crisp, clearly defined bands, are more desirable than those with a less distinct pattern. At a color level, the trend is toward pure colors — pure white and pure yellow in preference to cream yellow and off-white.

GROWTH RATE AND LONGEVITY IN CAPTIVITY

Fortunately for kingsnake owners, the moderate growth rate and ultimate size of kingsnakes is such that they will not quickly outgrow cage space nor pose handling problems for their owners. Animals raised in captivity and in ideal conditions can reach adult size in under three years, by which time they should be able to breed. If maintained and fed properly, hatchling kingsnakes should double in length and girth during their first year and achieve at least a further doubling of girth and length by the end of the second year. Thus, a California kingsnake (*L. g. californiae*), which is nine inches at birth should be eighteen inches after the first year and at least thirty six inches after the second year.

The longevity of common kingsnakes has largely become a measure of vastly improved husbandry techniques. The average life expectancy of a common kingsnake kept in optimal captive conditions ranges from 10 to 15 years. The maximum longevity up to this point for a captive common kingsnake is 23 years.

Selecting a Common Kingsnake

There is no doubt that captive-bred kingsnakes are one of the best selections for novice snake keepers. On the other hand, wild-caught kingsnakes can be difficult to handle and/or may have health problems that could require extensive treatment. So, select animals carefully when purchasing a wild-caught animal. You should also be informed of any state and federal laws that may regulate common kingsnakes which inhabit your area or state. A local pet store may be unaware of these laws. Most state laws do not differentiate between wild-caught and captive-bred animals.

SELECTING A HEALTHY KINGSNAKE

Even though there is ready availability of many different captive-bred varieties of kingsnakes which are <u>normally</u> quite healthy, all kingsnakes should be examined carefully before purchase. The following guidelines should allow you to select potentially healthy animals.

1. Before handling a potential acquisition, visually inspect it. Check to see that the body is well-rounded with no outlines of the ribs or backbones showing. Check to see that there are no depressions along the sides indicative of broken ribs. Check the skin for sores and scabs which may indicate the animal has been either roughly handled when collected or transported, or that it has been kept in poor conditions. While it is still resting in its enclosure, look to see whether the animal periodically opens its mouth as if it is having trouble breathing. This could indicate some sort of respiratory problem, whether by infection or parasites. Avoid "gaping" animals.

2. Have the animal handed to you. A healthy kingsnake, whether wild-caught or captive-bred, should feel strong and give an impression of good muscle tone when handled. Wild-caught kingsnakes tend to work their way out of your hands and when they're about half-way clear start wagging their bodies back and forth in big sweeps in

A speckled kingsnake *(Lampropeltis getula holbrooki)* from the area of Houston, Texas. Wild-caught specimens of this subspecies tend to be nervous and agressive. Photo by Brian Hubbs.

An adult albino (amelanistic) speckled kingsnake *(Lampropeltis getula holbrooki)*. The albino morph of this species is popular in the pet trade. Hatchlings feed readily on 1 - 2 day old mice. Photo by Robert Applegate.

South Florida kingsnake *(Lampropeltis getula "brooksi")*. An immature captive-bred specimen still showing distinct and clearly defined bands. These will fade as the animal becomes mature. Photo by Bill Love.

South Florida kingsnake *(Lampropeltis getula "brooksi")*. An adult wild-caught specimen collected near Brooks Canal. Photo by Bill Love.

order to get free. This may not seem like an endearing behavior but it certainly demonstrates a kingsnake's muscular vigor. Avoid animals that are sluggish and limp. This invariably indicates poor health.

3. With the animal still in hand there are a number of steps to perform, starting with the head, to determine health. First, have someone assist you by firmly holding the body of the snake while you hold it behind the head. Then, either by applying light downward pressure to the side of the lower jaw using the thumb, or by gently pulling down on the skin under the lower jaw, partially open the mouth of the snake. This is best done one side at a time. Look for the presence in the mouth of an unusual amount of mucus. Along the gum line and teeth line search for any red spots, lesions, or accumulations of caseous material (cheesy-looking matter). The presence of abundant or bubbly mucus is a very reliable indicator of a respiratory infection. The red spots very likely indicate the beginning of stomatitis (mouthrot). The cheesy-looking matter is a sure sign of advanced stomatitis. Animals with these symptoms should be avoided.

4. While still holding the head, check the eyes to make sure they are clear and free of any signs of cloudiness, damage, or injuries. If the snake happens to be in shed, both eyes should have the same amount of cloudiness. It may be a good idea to wait until after the animal has shed to complete your examination.

5. Allow the snake to "slide" between your hands. Using your fingertips, gently feel for unusual indents or lumps along the body. Avoid animals with these problems.

6. Check the underside of the snake (belly) for stained, damaged, or raised scales. These are probable signs of skin infections and animals with these symptoms should be avoided.

7. Mites are a very common problem in snakes, whether wild-caught or captive-bred, and any prospective addition to your collection should be thoroughly checked for these external parasites. Look for bead-like mites crawling on the snake or tiny white specks scattered

over the body. These specks are mite feces. Next check the edges of the eyes where mites can be imbedded between the rim and the eye itself. The presence of mites gives a raised impression to the eye rim. After looking for mites on the snake, closely inspect your hands to see if any tiny bead-like creatures are crawling about. The treatment of these parasites is never easy on the snake and the mites can readily spread throughout your collection. So, unless you are in need of that particular snake, you would do best to avoid an infected animal. See the section on Diseases for treatment.

8. Check for ticks. These are also external parasites, although much larger than mites. They look like flattened, round, nearly scale-like organisms which attach themselves between the scales nearly any-where on the body. These do not present the life-threatening problem that mites do, but they should be removed as soon the animal gets home.

9. Inspect around the opening to the cloaca (vent). Make sure the anal scale lies flat, is undamaged, and is free of any crusty substance. Make sure there is no smeared diarrhea on the surrounding area. Don't buy an animal with these symptoms.

Manually everting the hemipenes of a small snake. It is highly recommended that you seek the advice of an experienced herpetoculturist before attempting this procedure. If not properly performed, bleeding, crushing-type trauma and possibly skeletal damage may result. Photo by Chris Estep.

Speckled kingsnake *(Lampropeltis getula holbrooki).* An immature specimen from Kansas. Photo by Brian Hubbs.

Black kingsnake *(Lampropeltis getula nigra).* A wild-caught specimen from St. Clair County, Alabama. This subspecies is still collected in small numbers from the wild for the pet trade. Photo by Bill Love.

Acclimation of Wild-Caught Kingsnakes

Many wild-caught kingsnakes will acclimate to captive conditions within a relatively short time, although there can be many exceptions. With captive-bred animals the great majority will readily feed and adjust to captivity. The following steps should significantly increase the chances that your wild specimens do acclimate well to captivity.

1. When bringing a new snake home, put it in a quarantine situation by keeping it in a room isolated from the rest of your collection. Newly purchased snakes brought into an established collection could pose a serious health threat to your other reptiles. Ideally, quarantining of new animals should be done in a completely different room using easily monitored, cleaned, and disinfected enclosures. Newspaper is the best ground medium for this purpose. The materials and tools used for cleaning, etc., should be used on only one cage. Tools should be dipped in a disinfectant such as Unicide® or a 5% bleach solution if used with other animals or cages. Food items, cage furniture, etc., should not be transferred from one cage to another.

Probing a snake in order to determine its sex. This is a procedure which requires a certain amount of finesse. Ask an experienced individual to show you the right way to do this. This animal is a female. Photo by Chris Estep.

The quarantine period should last from eight to twelve weeks, depending on the health of the animals. Also, remember your own hygiene. Use disposable latex gloves, if possible, or at least use disinfectant after working on quarantined cages. Always wash with a disinfectant soap such as Betadine® scrub after maintenance of animals. A good maintenance protocol is to only deal with animals in the quarantine area at the end of the day when you will not need to return to your established collection.

2. With wild-collected animals, it is highly recommended that a stool check for parasites be performed by your reptile veterinarian. Obtain an estimate from a veterinarian as to the cost for a parasite check. In some cases veterinarians will charge an amount several times the cost of the animal for a thorough parasite check and treatment. If the cost is too high, consider a routine treatment for at least nematodes and flagellate protozoans. Most wild-caught snakes tend to be infested with at least one type of internal parasite which must be treated immediately. These may include nematodes (roundworms), trematodes (flukes), cestodes (tapeworms), pentastomes, and protozoans. If you don't have a reptile veterinarian, then your regular vet should at least be able to determine the general type of internal parasite infecting the snake, and the best course of treatment. If you can't or won't afford this treatment, then selecting a wild-caught animal may not be the best course of action.

3. Once home, the snake should be placed in an appropriate escape-proof enclosure with heat gradients, a water dish, and a shelter (see the section on Housing and Maintenance). Initially, leave the animal alone for two to three days. It shouldn't be handled except for parasite treatment or cage cleaning until it shows clear signs of adapting to captivity (feeding, gaining and maintaining weight, vigorous when active).

4. Any ticks should be removed as soon as possible by applying a drop of rubbing alcohol to the body of the tick. After a few minutes, firmly pull out the tick with a pair of tweezers.

5. After the initial settling-in period, proceed with the feeding steps described in the section entitled Feeding.

VARIATION IN THE CALIFORNIA KINGSNAKE

Coastal phase from Carlsbad, California. Photo by Brian Hubbs.

Wild-caught banded specimen with characteristics intermediate between the coastal and desert phases. Photo by Glen Carlzen.

Wild-caught coastal phase from San Diego county, California. Photo by Brian Hubbs.

Striped desert phase. This morph is seldom encountered in the wild and relatively few are produced in captivity. Photo by Glen Carlzen.

A specimen with an aberrant pattern. Photo by Glen Carlzen.

Immature Newport striped morph. Photo by Glen Carlzen.

HANDLING

One principal appeal of common kingsnakes is their docile disposition, either as captive-bred or wild-caught animals. Adult wild-caught common kingsnakes need to be handled often and on a consistent basis to keep them easily manageable. Wild-caught adults often tend to produce foul-smelling musk when first collected. With repeated handling, a snake will usually stop performing this offensive behavior. One subspecies of common kingsnake which, when collected, often exhibits defensive behavior is the speckled kingsnake (*L. g. holbrooki*). This subspecies will consistently coil and strike which will be accompanied by vigorous tail rattling. It will take a determined effort and regular gentle handling by a snake keeper for a nervous, aggressive snake to habituate to handling. Fortunately, when speckled kingsnakes are obtained as captive-bred babies or subadults, gentle handling on a regular schedule will eliminate any aggressive behavior. California kingsnakes (*L. g. californiae*) also have a reputation of being initially nippy.

Common kingsnakes move in a persistent and determined manner. Handling a subadult or adult entails using both hands to support the animal without trying to restrain its movements, essentially allowing it to move from hand to hand. Eventually the snake should calm down and you will be able to handle it with ease. Hatchlings tend to always be in motion and the safest way to handle them is with open hands for brief periods of time (no more than five minutes), preferably over a table top to prevent their falling to the floor. Once hatchlings get some size to them, especially girth, then regular, gentle handling can occur more frequently. When handling any snake, regardless of type, never let it coil around your neck or get near your face.

Sometimes a common kingsnake will be agitated when being handled and will perform the typical flight movements whereby it violently swings its body back and forth. If the animal does display this type of behavior, it is best to return it to its cage and try again another time. Excessive restraint when a snake performs this "flight" behavior can sometimes cause injuries.

Housing and Maintenance

SELECTING AN ENCLOSURE

Kingsnakes should be housed in enclosures specifically made for snakes. These include several different types of commercially constructed enclosures of either all glass with sliding screen tops, all fiberglass with sliding glass fronts which can be locked, or custom-made wood cages with framed-glass or plexiglass doors which can also be locked. Some professional colubrid breeders use a custom-built cage which has two separate compartments. The upper compartment has the water dish, one or two shelters, and can be accessed through a front-opening, locking, framed-glass door. The bottom compartment is actually a drawer which the snake can enter through a hole cut in the bottom of the upper compartment. This lower compartment acts as a hiding place and allows ease of cleaning. With this type of setup, pairs can readily be kept together. During feeding each animal is segregated in its own compartment by simply plugging the hole connecting the two compartments.

An alternative approach to the above-mentioned cages, one used by some commercial breeders, is to keep kingsnakes in large plastic storage containers of appropriate size. These are placed on shelving which is spaced in such a way as to allow no space between the top of the plastic lid and the bottom of the next shelf up. This arrangement allows for relatively inexpensive housing with good security against escapes. The key to this system is the spacing of the shelves and making sure the width of the shelf is at least as wide as the lid of the container. Of course every container housing a snake must have a shelf above it. For adult kingsnakes, the larger size plastic containers made by Rubbermaid® (26 quart) are recommended. When using plastic storage containers, adequate ventilation is critical, so make sure that several holes are drilled in each side (for softer semitranslucent plastic containers) or burned through using a soldering iron (for hard clear plastic containers). If a soldering iron is used, make sure you do this in a well ventilated area and avoid breathing any fumes. Hard plastic containers can easily crack if one uses a drill. Cages which are not specifically made to house snakes, such as all-glass aquariums with separate screen tops, are not escape proof and therefore are not recommended for most snakes, including kingsnakes, which are extremely good escape artists. So, be responsible and obtain the proper enclosure or build one to suit your needs. Do not make the selection of an enclosure secondary to your purchasing of a snake. There are hundreds, if not thousands, of stories of pet snakes escaping from inadequate enclosures. ("But honey, I really didn't forget to put the book back on top of the board on the kingsnake tank, honest.")

There is an ever-growing trend in local government to restrict the own-ership of any exotic animal, including reptiles. Every time a snake escapes and other people become aware of it, more fuel is added to the argument of those who favor restrictions. One must also think of neighbors who might overreact if confronted with a snake and take a shovel to the poor animal. You must be responsible for the sake of everyone keeping reptiles, so GET A CAGE WITH A PRO-PER LOCKING MECHANISM.

SIZE OF ENCLOSURE

Dimensions for the housing of hatchling kingsnakes should be no smaller than twelve inches long, six and a half inches wide, and three and a half inches deep. This size corresponds to the size of a two quart Rubbermaid® plastic container, which is also secure enough for juvenile kingsnakes. A ten gallon aquarium (20 inches x 10 inches) with a locking screen top also works well and is widely available in most pet stores. This size enclosure will work for most kingsnakes up to a year old.

For small adults, the cage should have a minimum floor surface area equal to that of a standard ten gallon aquarium (20 inches x 10 inches). A sixteen quart plastic Rubbermaid® storage container is also a good size for small adults.

For adult kingsnakes, the minimum size enclosure should be 24 inches long and 11 inches wide which corresponds to a twenty gallon high aquarium. Preferably, a 30 inch x 12 inch or larger enclosure should be used for the larger species.

Besides the strictly utilitarian enclosure, there is also the option of designing a naturalistic vivarium. Vivaria 29 gallon and up are recommended for this purpose. By using a more natural type of ground medium (see below), pieces of cork bark and/or driftwood, and possibly one of the various natural-looking shelters, you can create an attractive vivarium everyone will enjoy.

GROUND MEDIUM

There are several widely used ground media used for kingsnakes. Butcher paper and newspaper have very distinct advantages; they are cheap, somewhat absorbent, readily available, and very easy to change when soiled. They aren't attractive, but are very functional. During the acclimation stage, kingsnakes should be kept on paper to monitor their stools and to facilitate detection and treatment of a mite problem.

Once you are sure that the snake is acclimated, then other substrate materials can be used. The most popular are white pine shavings and shredded aspen which are sold in bulk as small animal bedding. Certain types of wood shavings which can contain harmful compounds (i.e., cedar and redwood) should be avoided. Some snake keepers have suggested that even pine shavings are potentially harmful because they can become lodged in the mouth when the snake is fed, thus possibly causing mouth disease. Keep a close watch for this problem.

A commercial snake enclosure with sliding glass front, manufactured by Neodesha Plastics. Photo by Chris Estep.

22

A number three aquarium gravel (not silica sand, but a smooth, fine, rounded gravel) will make an attractive, natural-looking, and easily changeable ground medium. Other herpetoculturists have used a fine grade aquarium silica sand which can be attractive in naturalistic desert-type vivaria. Europeans have also successfully used sandy soil mixes. Remember that the reason early herpetoculturists had poor success keeping snakes on soil is that they kept the soil surface wet. A key when keeping snakes on soil is to have a vivarium designed such that a significant portion of the upper crust of the soil is dry. This is similar to what happens in the wild in many areas where the sun essentially dries out the soil surface. The bottom line is that most snakes will not fare well if kept for prolonged periods of time on a damp substrate.

TEMPERATURE AND HUMIDITY

Common kingsnakes have such a wide distribution that generalized temperature ranges may at first seem inappropriate. The key is to provide a range of temperature gradients that will allow a snake to select the temperature which suits it best. A temperature gradient of 77 - 86°F will be suitable for all common kingsnakes. In addition, it is recommended that shelters be placed in both the warm and cool areas. Many kingsnake specialists feel that it is very important for the optimal health of the animals to provide a well-defined gradient. The nighttime temperature can be allowed to drop into the mid to low 70's (°F).

There are several types of reptile heaters now available which will work for kingsnakes. These include reptile heating pads which are either placed inside the cage or attached to the underside, and heating strips with built-in or added on thermostatic controls. Because king-snakes are rather secretive animals, incandescent light bulbs and fixtures are inappropriate and should not be used. This will also eliminate the possibility of thermal burns which happen all too often with incandescent heating.

It is essential that a thermometer be used to calibrate the cage temperature, regardless of which heating system is used. This will ensure that the surface area where the heat source is located is not overheated

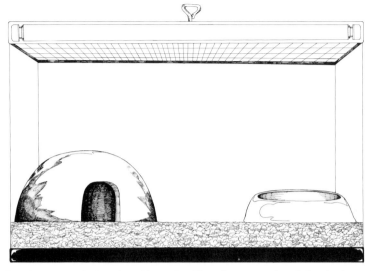

A bare bones setup for keeping a kingsnake. The substrate consists of pine shavings. A shelter and a water dish are provided. A heat strip or subtank heating pad should be used as a source of heat. Ideally, two shelters should be used, one over the cool area and oneover the heated area, to allow a snake access to security. A thermometer should be used to calibrate the heat. The enclosure has a sliding screen top with a pin to keep it securely locked. Illustration by Glenn Warren.

A shelf setup in which vivaria with screen tops slide. A heat strip controlled by a thermostat is placed in a routed depression underlying the tank. Many keepers place aluminum sheeting over heat stripts or heat tape to reduce or eliminate the risk of fire. Photo by Chris Estep.

(i.e, 86°F, not 95°F). Several different types of thermometers can be used. The best available are the electronic digital thermometers with an external probe that can be placed directly over the heat source of the enclosure. An inexpensive alternative is to use two of the adhesive strip-type thermometers, placing one on the cool end, the other on the warm end. Unfortunately, you will get a reading of the air temperature in the enclosure only, and not a direct reading from the heat source.

Do not under any circumstances use "hot rocks" without some way of controlling the heat output (i.e., rheostat or thermostat). Some of the hot rock or hot block-type heaters can burn you, as well as your snakes. If not used properly, the thermal burns these heating devices can cause could run up big vet bills, as well as seriously injure the snake. The surface temperature of some hot rocks reaches 105°F. Recently, hot rock-type heaters have been developed with a thermostatic control. Inquire about this product at your local pet store.

SHELTERS

Kingsnakes are relatively secretive animals. In the wild they tend to hide during the greater part of the day and exhibit similar behavior in captivity. An exception to this is during the breeding season when animals may be out looking for mates. Appropriate shelters must be provided that will restrict the amount of light and give them a sense of confinement. Two shelters should be placed in the vivarium, so that one is over the warm area and one is on the cool side of the enclosure.

There are now many different kinds of reptile shelters available in the pet trade which will work for kingsnakes. A natural and attractive shelter can be made from curled sections of cork bark which can be purchased from pet stores, reptile dealers, or sometimes plant nurseries. Some people use cardboard boxes, which will work but tend to be unsightly and disintegrate quickly. Also, cardboard is easily moved around by the snake itself, thus removing any sense of solidity and security. There are molded plastic, as well as formed concrete shelters, now offered in the pet trade which are attractive and will work well.

California kingsnake *(Lampropeltis getula californiae)*. Striped coastal phase. Photo by Glen Carlzen.

California kingsnake *(Lampropeltis getula californiae)*. Striped desert phase. Photo by Glen Carlzen.

Feeding

In the wild, kingsnakes feed on a wide variety of warm-blooded and cold-blooded prey. They can feed on warm-blooded prey such as mice and small rats, or they will eat a lizard or other snakes and even hatchling turtles. Because they are snake eaters they must be kept separately when young. It is as hatchlings and subadults that problems occur with cannibalism. As full grown adults this problem diminishes. However, it has been noted that desert-dwelling kingsnakes are more prone to eat other snakes. It has been speculated that on the coasts the climate is cooler and more humid and thus provides a better habitat for rodents. In the desert, there tend to be fewer rodents and more naturally occurring small species of snakes.

An interesting aspect of kingsnake feeding habits is the fact that they are immune to the venom of native American pit vipers (*Sistrurus, Crotalus,* and *Agkistrodon*), which they may include in their natural diet. They are one of the very few types of snakes that exhibit this immunity. Regardless of the prey captured, it is usually constricted and/or pressed against a hard surface, often a combination of both.

FEEDING HATCHLINGS

If captive-bred hatchlings have been selected, feeding is normally no problem. Many kingsnake breeders sell their hatchlings only after they have started feeding. Hatchling kingsnakes will usually start to feed a few days to a few weeks after their first shed (some start before shedding). Make sure that each animal is housed separately and that they are provided with a shelter and a small container of water.

The best, most convenient initial food item for a hatchling is a one- to two-day-old mouse. One nice feature of keeping common kingsnakes of all sizes in captivity is that, in general, they will readily feed on prekilled mice, whether fresh or frozen. Frozen newborn mice (pinkies), as well as fuzzies and adults, are often available from pet stores that sell reptiles. Allow the mouse to warm to room temperature before introducing it into a cage. DO NOT put frozen mice in the microwave to thaw them out. What often happens in this case is that the mouse will explode. To speed thawing, soak the mice in hot water or place them a few inches from an incandescent light, but don't get them so hot that they cook.

Hatchling and subadult kingsnakes should be fed one to two mice every two to seven days, depending on the desired rate of growth. As a rule, snakes will grow faster if offered smaller food items two or more times a week, rather than a single larger food item once a week. First of all, smaller food items are easier to digest. Secondly, over a given period of time snakes fed smaller food items every two to three days will be able to consume a greater amount of food. In the winter months the feeding schedule can be reduced, although until kingsnakes reach breeding size most herpetoculturists aim for a rapid and steady growth rate. It is not uncommon, however, for juvenile kingsnakes to spontaneously go off feed for varying periods of time during the winter months. To continue obtaining a good growth rate, make sure that you keep the temperature gradients within the recommended range for maintenance and offer food frequently. A snake that refuses food on a given day may decide to feed on another.

Usually within any given clutch, there will be one or more stubborn or picky feeders. Before trying alternate methods, one should explore all the variations of offering pink mice: live, prekilled, prekilled and washed to remove scent, prekilled with brain matter smeared on the head and anterior part of the body. The latter method sounds gruesome but we are talking of a dead mouse and the method works surprisingly often. If the above methods fail, a well-proven trick to get reluctant kingsnake hatchlings started on pinkies is to rinse a prekilled mouse in water, dry it off, and then rub it against the skin of a lizard. This is called "scenting." Other methods of scenting include putting a piece of lizard (prekilled) tail in the mouth of a prekilled pink mouse or cutting a piece of skin from a prekilled feeder lizard and sticking it on the head of the prekilled mouse. Fence lizards (*Sceloporus*) are ideal animals to use for this purpose as they are a natural food for many kingsnakes. However, most commonly available lizards, including green anoles, will provide the scent necessary to trigger a feeding response. If the snake still refuses to feed on pink mice, then a feeder lizard should be tried. Most pet stores will sell an inexpensive lizard that should work. The key here is to

A California kingsnake *(Lampropeltis getula californiae)* feeding on a mouse. Photo by Robert Applegate.

Florida kingsnake *(Lampropeltis getula floridana)*. An immature specimen photographed in the wild. This subspecies is abundant and still collected for the pet trade. Photo by Bill Love.

obtain the smallest animal possible that can be easily swallowed. Slightly raising (3-5°F) the ambient air temperature in which the snake is kept may also stimulate a feeding response. If for some reason nothing seems to work, then force feeding will be the last resort.

To force feed a hatchling, gently hold the snake behind the head with thumb and forefinger while holding the rest of the body down on a solid, stable surface. Ideally, a prekilled newborn mouse should be used (the smaller the better). If you cannot obtain a day-old mouse or if a snake is unusually small then a section of leg or section of tail from a weaned, prekilled mouse can be used. If a mouse leg is used, make sure there are no bones sticking out through the skin or where it was separated from the body. With your free hand holding round-tipped forceps, grab the pinkie or mouse leg, lubricate it with water, and insert it head first or thigh-end first into the snake's mouth. With the mouse tail, insert the thick end first so the bristly hair lies flat as the tail is inserted. Force feeding a tail is probably the less stressful to the snake of the two. Often, if the section of leg or tail is inserted just past the throat and the snake is placed immediately back in its cage and left undisturbed, it will proceed to swallow the section on its own. If it regurgitates, you may have to repeat the procedure, gently pushing the section well past the throat area as far as the first third of the body. Most reluctant feeders, in the case of common kingsnakes, will begin to feed on their own after two or three force feedings.

SUBADULTS

As a kingsnake grows, the size of the prey offered will have to be increased accordingly. A good general rule is for the prey item to have a girth equal or up to one and a quarter times the apparent girth (to the naked eye) of the snake. Thus, hatchlings will graduate from hairless mice, to fuzzy mice (eyes closed but hair starting to grow), to just-weaned mice, and so on. As with hatchlings, one to two mice per feeding should be adequate. Until kingsnakes reach breeding size (approximately two years), they should continue to be fed every two to seven days. The growth rate should be rapid up to two or three years, but will begin to taper off after breeding size is reached.

ADULTS

Adult kingsnakes should be fed adult mice or just-weaned rats (for larger animals) on a regimen which will be determined by their breeding schedule (see section entitled Breeding). For those not interested in breeding, but just in keeping kingsnakes as pets, a feeding schedule of one to three adult mice (body girth equal to 1 and 1/4 times that of snake) per week per adult snake will be adequate. The number of mice used will have to be determined in part by the appearance of the snake and by its size. A large eastern kingsnake or Florida kingsnake will become quite lean on just a one-mouse-a-week diet. The diet will have to be adjusted so that the snake maintains a smooth rounded body without the outline of the ribs or backbone being prominent. As a general rule, kingsnakes four feet or more will require at least two adult mice a week to maintain good weight.

FEEDING REGIMEN FOR BREEDING KINGSNAKES

For those of you who hibernate your kingsnakes to condition them for breeding, you will have to stop all feeding 10-15 days prior to cooling. This is a necessary precaution to allow the snake to empty its digestive system. Most herpetoculturists prepare their kingsnakes for breeding sometime in November or December, partially depending on when temperatures drop enough to allow cooling of a "hibernation" room where snakes are maintained.

Upon return to normal temperatures following a cooling period (usually in March), kingsnakes can be placed back on a normal feeding schedule. Herpetoculturists usually wait a few days to a week before beginning to offer food. With most subspecies (speckled kings, which breed early, are an exception), you have an interval of a few weeks during which kingsnakes will readily feed before they actually begin breeding. The first or second shed of the female after removal from hibernation is often associated with the actual onset of the breeding period. If a snake is a little thin following removal from hibernation, it is important that you feed more frequent, somewhat smaller meals during this prebreeding "window" to allow it to reach an adequate weight. This can be critical to your breeding success.

During breeding, males will often be so frenzied that they may not feed readily (they have their priorities). Following copulations and as gestation progresses, female kingsnakes will typically feed less frequently and sometimes go off feed altogether. The key to continuous feeding of females is to offer smaller prey more frequently. One of the reasons that female snakes feed less frequently when gravid appears to be linked to the fact that developing eggs take up increasingly more room in the abdominal cavity. Large food items which create a large lump and a large fecal mass will often be refused during this time, while smaller food items will be accepted. Gravid female kingsnakes that are going off feed should be offered one or two fuzzy mice, early stage fuzzy rats, or large pink rats frequently. Do not offer inordinately large numbers of food items or you will cause the female to regurgitate. A small number of smaller-than-normal food items offered frequently (every two to three days) is the right course of action. It is important to keep gravid females on an optimal feeding regimen during the breeding period, not only to prevent any significant depletion of body weight, but also to help stimulate egg production for another clutch. According to Robert Applegate, a well-known and successful colubrid breeder, feedings during this time can make the difference between a single clutch and a second clutch of eggs. Male kingsnakes, on the other hand, usually need little or no inducement to feed at any time except when in shed, although many males may stop feeding when they are in close proximity to females during the breeding season. If this happens, try putting the male in a separate room, if possible, until it starts feeding again. The feeding schedule for males should be similar to that of females during the breeding season. Just be observant that your male does not become overweight. If this happens, gradually reduce the meals to one or two food items per meal. A feeding schedule of two to four adult mice should be initiated for a female immediately after she has deposited her eggs.

Diseases and Disorders

Both wild-caught and captive-bred kingsnakes can exhibit a number of diseases or disorders. These are often the result of environmental stress, improper maintenance, or the introduction of new animals into an established collection. Careful attention to vivarium design, temperature, and husbandry procedures will be important to minimize stress. Any new animals should be put in quarantine, checked for parasites (both internal or external) and treated accordingly before being introduced into a collection.

The following are some of the more common problems and their recommended treatments.

EXTERNAL PARASITES
TICKS
Wild-caught animals sometimes will have ticks imbedded in their skin. To remove a tick, apply a drop or two of rubbing alcohol to the body of a tick using a cotton swab. After five minutes, the tick will be easily removed with tweezers. If there are several ticks to be removed, then apply a pyrethrin-based spray to a cloth and wipe the snake with it. Later the dead ticks will drop off or will be easily removed. When using pyrethrin-containing products, make sure that you rinse the animal in lukewarm water after the treatment is completed. It has been suggested that pyrethrins, when misused, can cause respiratory problems and can damage the lens of the eye.

MITES
For any reptile keeper mites are a scourge. Once introduced into a collection, they are very difficult to get rid of. Therefore, it is extremely important to treat animals immediately, and preferably in quarantine.

Mites when present can usually be seen as tiny, dark, bead-like creatures moving about on the surface of a snake. Sometimes very tiny mites (ones that are young) appear much lighter. They are easier to spot when the snake is about to shed as this displaces them temporarily. A good indicator of mites is the presence of tiny white specks on the skin surface of a snake. These are usually mite feces and will cause a snake to appear covered with white dust when large numbers of mites are present. Pyrethrin sprays are very effective in eliminating them. Cages and cage contents can also be treated with pyrethrins. It is best to use a cloth dampened with the spray and wiped on the skin of the snake. Leave it on the animal for ten to twenty minutes before rinsing it off. Repeat the treatment in two to three weeks. A very effective method of treatment that has been somewhat controversial, but is widely used, is the use of pest strips impregnated with 2.2 dichlorovinyl dimethyl phosphate. Damage to internal organs, especially the liver, has been linked to misuse through overexposure. A piece of strip one inch wide by two inches long is enough to kill mites on kingsnakes in most enclosures. The piece should be put in some sort of perforated container so that there is no direct contact with the snake. Depending on the type of cage, air circulation should be cut to a minimum during treatment, which should last between twelve and twenty-four hours. Veterinarians have access to products for mite treatment that are relatively safe and effective, sometimes for long periods of time. One of these is an Ivermectin® solution in spray form to be applied topically.

Another safe method for killing mites is to sprinkle Sevin® (carbaryl) dust, available in nurseries and supermarkets, on newspaper at the bottom of a cage. This will kill mites within 24 hours. The treatment should be repeated in 10-12 days. The cage and surroundings should be disinfected at the time of both treatments for mites not to reoccur.

Don't forget that a mite infestation not only occurs on the snake but also on the cage contents, and on both the inside and outside surfaces of the cage. The entire cage and all of its contents need to be disinfected with household bleach. Cage contents that cannot be disinfected should be thrown out and replaced. The surrounding area should also be wiped with pyrethrins or at least a bleach solution. Remember, the reason mites often come back after treatment is that most products do not kill the mite eggs that lie at the bottom of a cage or on cage furniture. To successfully treat mites in a collection you must also treat/disinfect the enclosures. Obviously, these parasites are a major headache and should be prevented from being introduced into a collection. A thorough inspection of the snake prior to purchase, and quarantining newly purchased snakes, are highly recommended procedures.

INTERNAL PARASITES

All wild-collected kingsnakes should ideally have a fresh stool sample analyzed by a veterinarian. This is a relatively simple and inexpensive procedure in most cases, but get an estimate beforehand. A veterinarian will be able to prescribe an effective treatment protocol if there is a problem.

The following are some recommended treatments for internal parasites.

For nematodes (roundworms)
Thibenzole® (Thiabendazole), given orally at a dosage of 50-100 mg/kg. Repeat twice, two weeks apart, for a total of three treatments.

Panicur® (Fenbendazole), given orally at a dosage of 50-100 mg/kg. Repeat twice, two weeks apart, for a total of three treatments.

For cestodes (tapeworms)
Yomesan® (Niclosamide), given orally at a dosage of 150 mg/kg.

For pentastomes (lungworms)
Levamisole hydrochloride injectable at a dosage of 5 mg/kg.

For protozoans (*Entamoeba, Giardia, Trichomonas*, etc.)
Flagyl® (metronidazole), given orally at a dosage of 50 mg/kg for most protozoans, except *Entamoeba*, which may require double that dosage. Repeat in two weeks.

INFECTIOUS STOMATITIS (MOUTHROT):
Although mouthrot is not very common in kingsnakes, whether wild-caught or captive-bred, it does occasionally turn up in specimens kept in collections over time. Mouth injuries often predispose a snake to

mouthrot. Watch carefully for the early warning signs in snakes with injured mouths.

Mouthrot is a bacterial infection which attacks the tissue of the gums and symptoms will vary depending upon the severity of the infection. Swelling along the jawline and reluctance to feed are the early symptoms noticed by most snake keepers. An examination of the inside of the mouth will reveal an accumulation of caseous (cheesy-looking) matter along the gumline. In its early stages, mouthrot can easily be treated topically at home. The caseous matter should be gently removed using cotton swabs soaked in a 3% hydrogen peroxide solution or a mild mouthwash solution (three parts water to one part mouthwash). The author has had good success with Viadent® mouthwash which contains Sanguinaria extract, an herb known for its healing properties. Don't forget that the animal is stressed from this disease, so don't try to remove all the caseous substance at one time if a large area is affected. Work on it a little at a time. Betadine® solution (povidone-iodine) or Viadent® should be applied to the affected area at least on a daily basis. A spray bottle can be used to administer the Betadine® or Viadent®. This disease is highly infectious so you must disinfect yourself as well as all tools used during treatment. With conscientious treatment, the problem should clear up in two to three weeks. Serious cases will require consulting a veterinarian so that injectable antibiotics can be administered.

It has been suggested that a vitamin C deficiency may make an animal more susceptible to the development of stomatitis. Many snake keepers and breeders make sure their rodents have some vitamin C in their system, primarily by feeding mice soon after removal from their rearing containers. Mice fed or prekilled at this point will have vitamin C contained in a high quality rodent chow stored in their gut.

SKIN DISORDERS
SHEDDING PROBLEMS
The most common skin disorder involves the inability of the snake to shed its skin, whether in one piece or in several pieces. As most snake keepers know, a healthy snake usually sheds its skin in one

piece. A problem shed will be characterized by shed skin remaining attached to the body, including eye caps.

The most common cause of a problem shed is the lack of a water bowl large enough for the snake to soak in. Another possible cause is low relative air humidity. Certain diseases such as skin infections or mite infestations can also cause shedding problems. Usually a snake will shed within the first week following the clearing of opaque condition (skin and eyes with a diluted, milky white, and clouded appearance). If the snake fails to shed within this time period, you should consider soaking it to soften its old skin and facilitate shedding.

The usual course of treatment when a snake has a problem shed is to place the snake in a plastic storage box, with holes for aeration, in which a small amount of water, equal to approximately half the diameter (thickness) of the snake's body, has been placed. The lid is placed back on and secured with strong tape, unless one has the custom-made shelving flush with the top of the box. The snake is then allowed to soak for approximately 12 hours. The remaining shed may have come off by then as a result of the activity of the snake. If not, the shed skin will be easily removed by hand, gently pulling or slipping it off. There are also products now available in pet stores which aid in the removal of old skin from snakes.

Removing old eye caps is a delicate procedure which requires round-tipped tweezers and steady hands. The first step should be to soak the animal in a container that has a wet foam rubber sponge in it and that the snake can't get out of. A few hours of soaking should be enough to soften the eye caps to the point where they can be easily removed. After soaking, holding the snake behind the head, look for the edge of the eye cap along the rim of the eye. You may be able to gently lift it up with the edge of a fingernail. Once the edge has been found, use the round-tipped tweezers to gently pull the eye cap off. If the eye cap cannot easily be removed you may be able to wait until the next shed, making sure to soak the snake so that it readily sheds in one piece. Caution is advised when removing eye caps so that no damage is done to the cornea, which will lead to serious problems. If there is any doubt, consult an experienced snake keeper or a veterinarian.

A Florida kingsnake *(Lampropeltis getula floridana)* with skin blister disease. This is usually the result of keeping snakes on a substrate that is too wet or fouled, for extended periods of time. Photo by Glen Carlzen.

An original wild-collected striped albino California kingsnake *(Lampropeltis getula californiae),* from San Diego county, California. Photo by David Travis.

SKIN BLISTER DISEASE

This disease looks like little white bumps under the scales which causes them to rise. Normally the associated cause is a cage which is kept too wet or one that combines old feces and a wet ground medium. Either way, poor maintenance practices will allow for the bacteria which produce the problem to develop. The initial step is to put the animal in a clean, dry cage on clean ground medium and use a small water dish that does not allow for soaking. Wipe the snake with a warm wet cloth to remove any dirt or foreign substance. In addition, topical application of Betadine® solution to the skin with a cloth on a daily basis is recommended. If the disease seems extensive, then a veterinarian needs to be consulted and antibiotics administered. Recovery will not be complete until the next shed.

RODENT BITES

There really isn't any reason for bites to occur since kingsnakes readily accept prekilled rodents. This approach is certainly more humane for the rodent and safer for the snake.

Treatment of a rodent bite usually starts with cleansing the area with Betadine® solution and removing any loose skin or tissue. Applying a topical antibacterial ointment such as Neosporin® will usually be all that is necessary for full recovery. If the wound has become infected and an injectable antibiotic is needed, a veterinarian should be consulted. The author has had good results with Baytril® (enrofloxacin) at a dosage of 20 mg/kg administered once a day for five days.

RESPIRATORY INFECTIONS

Respiratory infections may occur in kingsnakes that are kept at intermediate temperatures; too cool for normal activity and effective digestion and too warm to induce the state of metabolic rest usually associated with hibernation. Other factors including poor state of health will increase susceptibility to respiratory infections.

In the earliest stages of a respiratory infection the symptoms are usually decreased activity, reluctance to feed and, when the inside of the mouth is examined, the presence of increased mucus and often bubbly mucus. As the disease progresses into pneumonia, the a-mount of mucus increases, sometimes emerging through the sides of the mouth. The snake will gape as it struggles to breath and it will exhale forcibly. In the early stages, maintaining the snake at uniformly higher temperatures of 86-90°F around the clock will usually allow a snake's immune system to fight off the infection. If the disease worsens or demonstrates clear symptoms of pneumonia, a veterinarian should be consulted and injectable antibiotics administered.

One should be aware of other causes of respiratory diseases. In wild-collected kingsnakes high parasite loads and particularly lungworms can cause respiratory distress that results in gaping. Another cause is allergic reactions to such things as the substrate medium and, more commonly, a reaction to ammonia gas released by accumulating feces in an enclosure that is too wet. Many a herpetoculturist upon opening a fouled cage has been struck by the strong ammonia smell. Long-term exposure to this gas can affect a snake's respiratory system.

GASTROINTESTINAL INFECTIONS
Any kingsnake that refuses food or regularly regurgitates food and also has diarrhea or discolored or unusually smelly or bloody stools should be taken to a veterinarian to determine the cause. Untreated snakes with these symptoms usually die. On the other hand, with proper diagnosis and treatment the prognosis for a cure and long-term survival is usually good. Any snake with the above symptoms should be quarantined and strict procedures adopted to make sure that one doesn't infect other animals in a collection. These procedures should include a thorough washing of hands with a disinfectant following any maintenance or handling of the infected snake, not using any tools used for the maintenance of this snake with other snakes, disinfecting these tools in a bleach solution after use, and performing the maintenance of any sick snakes at the end of one's maintenance schedule so one does not have to maintain or handle healthy snakes after one has maintained sick animals.

Eastern kingsnake *(Lampropeltis getula getula).* A wild-caught specimen from Jaspar County, South Carolina. Photo by Bill Love.

Eastern kingsnake *(Lampropeltis getula getula).* A specimen with an odd zigzag pattern. Photo by Bill Love.

VISUAL ASSESSMENT OF HEALTH

Routine visual inspection of your snake should be an integral part of your husbandry techniques. The following steps should be used on a daily basis to help prevent serious ailments.

1. Muscle tone/vigor - Does the snake move about the cage in an easy manner? Are there any depressed areas on the body? When the snake is picked up does it feel strong and vigorous in its movements or does it feel kind of sluggish?
2. Assess the weight of your snake. Can you see the backbone or ribs through the skin even though the snake eats well?
3. Eyes, mouth and vent - Do the eyes appear to be clear and alert without being sunken in? Are there any lumps, bumps, or bruises on or around the mouth? Is the vent area clean and free of any caked or runny fecal matter?
4. Fecal assessment - Do the feces appear firm with proper color, or watery, off-color, or terribly foul smelling?
5. Behavior - Is the snake gaping its mouth? Does it appear to have a loss of equilibrium, to be listless, or ceaselessly move about the cage?

If any of the above problems are seen, a visit to the veterinarian is recommended or consultation of reference manuals or with other herpetoculturists should be made to assess the possible cause of the problem. Runny stools, blood in the stools or unusual weight loss should almost always be investigated through a fecal analysis, a procedure best performed by a qualified veterinarian. A daily visual check of your snake's cage will also help eliminate potential health risks. Make sure substrate material is clean and dry, cage furniture is secure, and water and water bowls are clean. Any shed skin should be removed along with any fecal material.

An Overview of the Common Kingsnake (*Lampropeltis getula*)

The following are the seven recognized (by herpetologists) and six unrecognized (except by herpetoculturists) subspecies of the common kingsnake.

CALIFORNIA KINGSNAKE (*Lampropeltis getula californiae*)
This is a highly variable subspecies and is available in several colors and forms. They range from the tip of the Baja peninsula north to southern Oregon and from the west coast of California east to desert areas of Nevada and Arizona. The geographical variants established in herpetoculture include pattern morphs and color morphs.

The most widely recognized pattern morphs are: striped, banded, aberrant (variable but sometimes consistent pattern variations that don't fit the striped or pattern categories), patternless (chocolate), Newport Beach, ones characterized by the relative width of light banding or a high percentage of light coloration and reduction of dark coloration, and most recently, the development of a patternless albino (snow king). Other geographical variants are likely to be isolated in herpetoculture in the future and selectively bred. There are often consistencies in pattern and color of California kingsnakes from specific areas, allowing for a considerable degree of typing by herpetoculturists and segregation in breeding programs.

The color morphs are: normal phase color, characterized by varying degrees of light yellow bands or stripes; desert phase, distinguished by pure white bands or stripes; and at least three kinds of amelanistic albinos. Standard albinos, lavender with ruby red eyes, and recently a lavender and bright yellow strain with red eyes are some of the albino morphs currently available.

Some of the most attractive forms of the California kingsnake can be found in the Mojave Desert and in parts of Baja, California where specimens possess extra wide white bands. In other parts of Baja, these snakes tend towards melanism and become the "conjuncta" and "nitida" morphs of herpetoculture. The "nitida" morph is commonly called the Baja or Cape kingsnake and is bluish black with only the faintest hint of banding or striping.

FLORIDA KINGSNAKE (*Lampropeltis getula floridana*)
The Florida kingsnake is generally brown with yellowish color on each scale. A good indicator of the Florida subspecies is the many crossbands of light scales which extend down the back. This subspecies is not often captive-bred. However, wild-caught specimens are regularly offered for sale. Actually, these snakes are heavily collected in the sugar cane fields south of Lake Okeechobee. The large population there is due solely to man's manipulation of the habitat in that area. These snakes are almost never collected from their natural habitat (glades, pine lands, and open grassland) because of the ease of collection in the sugarcane fields.

On an interesting note, the Florida Fish and Game Department is conducting a survey of all breeders of native Florida reptiles and amphibians. The Department has a genuine concern for population decline in all genera of reptiles and amphibians. However, the author believes that except for *L.g. floridana*, all other native Florida kingsnakes are rarely collected and that the great majority offered for sale are captive-bred. Hopefully, this study will become public and the Department won't take any hasty actions, such as complete protection of all the native fauna. In the case of the common Florida kingsnake, there is reason to believe that the population could increase to the point of overpopulation near Lake Okeechobee. This would be counterproductive in terms of conservation. Fortunately, there is a united group of professionals and serious hobbyists in Florida that is politically active and can affect some decisions by the Department.

Eastern kingsnake *(Lampropeltis getula getula).* **An unusually attractive specimen from Leon County, Florida. Photo by Bill Love.**

Outer Banks kingsnake *(Lampropeltis getula "sticticeps").* **This morph from the Outer Banks of North Carolina is possibly the rarest form of the common kingsnakes in captivity. Photo by Bill Love.**

California kingsnake *(Lampropeltis getula californiae).* A half banded and half striped specimen, caught in the Carlsbad area of California. Photo by Brian Hubbs.

California kingsnake *(Lampropeltis getula californiae).* A wild-caught specimen from San Diego county, California. Photo by Brian Hubbs.

EASTERN KINGSNAKE (*Lampropeltis getula getula*)
This subspecies is alternately called the chain kingsnake because of the distinct pattern of connected, light-colored crossbands extending down the back. The eastern kingsnake ranges from s. New Jersey to n. Florida. This subspecies is seldom captive-bred, but adults sometimes appear in pet or specialty stores. For the most part, it is uncommon in herpetoculture and becoming uncommon in the wild, mostly due to habitat destruction. Increased efforts need to be made to establish pure forms, not intergrades, in the trade. A black patternless specimen of the eastern kingsnake is currently in captivity and may become available in the future. This is the largest member of the genus with an impressive record length of eighty-four inches.

The greatest concentration of these snakes occurs from Virginia to Georgia. Although these two states have protected them, North and South Carolina have not, and significant numbers continue to be collected. The regular availability of wild-caught specimens may in part account for the general lack of interest in developing them for commercial herpetoculture.

SPECKLED KINGSNAKE (*Lampropeltis getula holbrooki*)
The speckled kingsnake is so named because of its scale pattern. It has a cream-to-yellow spot on each of the dark brown or black scales which covers the whole back of the snake. It is a truly beautiful animal. Unfortunately, wild-caught specimens tend to be ill-tempered, although captive-bred animals, which are usually available, prove to be good captives. An albino form has been developed by herpetoculturists and is regularly available. Its range is from s. Iowa to the Gulf of Mexico and west to eastern Texas.

BLACK KINGSNAKE (*Lampropeltis getula nigra*)
Although this subspecies is referred to as the black kingsnake, it usually does have some pattern. This consists of greatly reduced light spots which may form slight bands across the back or just show a random light speckling down the back and sides. The ventral color is mostly black with intermittent white patches. It ranges from s. Ohio down to central Alabama. This subspecies is rarely seen in pet stores and is even relatively uncommon in reptile specialty stores,

Desert kingsnake *(Lampropeltis getula spendida).* **An unusually attractive wild-caught specimen from Texas. Photo by Brian Hubbs.**

Juvenile blotched kingsnake *(Lampropeltis getula "goini").* **This strain selectively bred by a few hobbyists retains a considerable amount of orange when adult. Photo by Bill Love.**

either wild-caught or captive-bred. There are, however, several people in the U.S. who have successful breeding programs.

MEXICAN BLACK KINGSNAKE (*Lampropeltis getula nigrita***)**
The pure form (no intergradation with other overlapping kingsnake subspecies) of the Mexican black kingsnake is usually all black or very dark brown, even the scales on the underside. Hatchlings sometimes will show a bit of a pattern while the adults occasionally show some light spots along the sides. Its range is limited to northwestern Mexico and a small area in southern Arizona. Availability is still limited, although a number of herpetoculturists have had success breeding them.

DESERT KINGSNAKE (*Lampropeltis getula splendida***)**
This is the desert kingsnake which ranges from central Texas through southern and central New Mexico and into southern Arizona. It has a dark brown to black background color with numerous yellow or white spots on the sides. The lighter-colored scales form many thin bands across the back. Being from hot, dry areas, it is normally nocturnal, although it can be found during the day near arroyos and dry washes after late spring rains. The author has found this snake in southern Arizona in just these conditions. Wild-caught desert kingsnakes can often be found in local pet stores, in the areas where they occur, but captive-bred babies are becoming more readily available to the general public.

NO LONGER RECOGNIZED SUBSPECIES
There are some types of kingsnakes that were once recognized by herpetologists as separate subspecies, but are no longer. *L. getula* has been revised a number of times with the most recent version favoring a reduction in the number of recognized subspecies. This is not to say that the unrecognized subspecies are not valued by herpetoculturists. On the contrary, these kingsnakes are highly prized and are being bred in their pure forms. Herpetoculturists place great emphasis on geographical and phenotypic variations of kingsnakes and have, in many cases, preserved the unique traits of various wild populations of *Lampropeltis*. This has been achieved through meticulous management of captive-bred populations. As a result, many herpeto-

culturists have chosen to retain subspecific names currently considered obsolete by the scientific community. This practice serves to represent and to segregate these respective *Lampropeltis* in the pet trade. In addition, the segregation of these morphs is desirable, especially when genetic lines from specific geographical areas are preserved (perhaps even ones that are threatened with destruction).

Note: To indicate that the unrecognized subspecies are herpetocultural forms rather than subspecies recognized in herpetology, the author has chosen to list the herpetocultural subspecies in quotes.

SOUTH FLORIDA KINGSNAKE *(Lampropeltis getula "brooksi")*

The south Florida kingsnake is considered by herpetologists to be only a variety of the Florida kingsnake (*Lampropeltis g. floridana*). *"Brooksi"* is also known as the peninsula kingsnake, and as the golden phase of the Florida kingsnake, for good reason. A good *"brooksi"* has very little dark color to the scales, with most being tan to yellowish. There is almost no pattern in adults, although juveniles do show distinctive banding. This subspecies is only found in extreme southern Florida. It inhabits hammocks and glades, as well as fields, and can reach a length of sixty inches.

BAJA BANDED KINGSNAKE *(Lampropeltis getula "conjuncta")*

See California kingsnake.

THE BLOTCHED KINGSNAKE (*Lampropeltis getula "goini"*)

Lampropeltis getula "goini" is known as the blotched kingsnake and only occurs in the Florida panhandle (northwest part of the state) in the Chipola and Apalachicola River valleys. Herpetologists consider these kingsnakes to be *Lampropeltis g. getula* and *Lampropeltis g. floridana* intergrades. The bands are very wide, reduced in number, and are made of tan scales with dark dots in the middle of each one. The alternating dark bands may or may not have tan dots in the middle of each scale. The effect is quite attractive. The adults can reach a length of sixty inches. The following morphs are currently being bred by herpetoculturists: blotched, reverse patterned, striped, and

A melanistic California kingsnake *(Lampropeltis getula californiae)*. This morph is characterized by the lack of pattern. Photo by David Travis.

Baja kingsnake *(Lampropeltis getula "nitida")*. These are now produced in small numbers by herpetoculturists. Photo by Glen Carlzen.

Blotched kingsnake *(Lampropeltis getula "goini")*. A captive-bred specimen, lineated and speckled. Photo by Bill Love.

Blotched kingsnake *(Lampropeltis getula "goini" x Lampropeltis getula getula)*. An intergrade from southern Georgia. Photo by Bill Love.

patternless. There is a speckled form and a striped form which occur in nature. In fact, there is some well-founded speculation that these forms are the true *"goini"* and that the blotched form is an intergrade. The centuries of man's impact on the habitat of these snakes, along with geographical transformation, may have allowed intergradation to occur.

BAJA or CAPE KINGSNAKE *(Lampropeltis getula "nitida")*
See California kingsnake.

OUTER BANKS KINGSNAKE *(Lampropeltis getula "sticticeps")*
The Outer Banks kingsnake is from the islands off the coast of North Carolina. It is distinguished by light-colored scales forming short bands across the back on a dark brown to black background. The bands do not extend around the body of the snake to meet the ventral scales on the bottom. The top of the head and the labials usually have numerous white markings. Adults can reach a length of fifty inches. It is believed that *Lampropeltis g. "sticticeps"* is an intergrade between *Lampropeltis g. getula* and *Lampropeltis g. floridana*. However, it is well documented that *floridana* does not occur as far north as *getula*. It is speculated by some that this intergradation occurred in the distant past when perhaps *L. g. floridana* did range that far north while others are skeptical of this intergradation theory. Whichever theory is correct, the Outer Banks kingsnake is an uncommon and beautiful snake that is rare in collections and seldom available as a captive-bred animal.

YUMA KINGSNAKE *(Lampropeltis getula "yumensis")*
This is a subspecies that was once widely recognized, but is no longer. The wild-caught specimens found in its range superficially resemble the banded desert-phase of *L. g. californiae*. The differences the author has seen are that the bands are narrower and more numerous and there is much less white on the head. There is some conjecture that this is an intergrade between *L. g. californiae* and *L. g. splendida*.

Breeding

GENERAL INFORMATION

All kingsnakes are oviparous, meaning that they lay eggs which develop and hatch outside of the female's body. In the wild, common kingsnakes breed between March and June. Captive kingsnakes, with proper conditioning, will readily breed during the same months as wild kingsnakes, although some breeders manipulate the cooling cycle so that breeding is spread out over a greater period of time. Common kingsnakes in captivity will typically breed within a few weeks following removal from hibernation and return to a normal maintenance schedule. The first or second shed by a female following removal from hibernation is associated with sexual readiness and the production of pheromones which play a key role in the successful copulation of common kingsnakes. Following copulation, a female kingsnake will usually lay eggs four to eight weeks later, although that time interval could extend to as much as twelve weeks. The clutch sizes of common kingsnakes will range anywhere from three to twenty-four, with the average number of eggs per clutch in the low- to mid-teens. The size of a female, its age, health, and genetic factors will play a key role in the number of eggs a female may produce. Many common kingsnakes, when larger and if provided with enough food, will lay two clutches of eggs during the breeding season. The incubation of kingsnake eggs usually lasts from six to ten weeks, possibly longer, depending on incubation temperature. Newborn kingsnakes are from eight to thirteen inches long and usually shed within their first week.

BEFORE BREEDING KINGSNAKES

There are certain considerations that need to be addressed before attempting to breed kingsnakes. First, you must have at least one sexual pair of animals. If uncertain about the sex of your animals, have them sexed by an experienced herpetoculturist. The next consideration is the age of your snakes. Successful breeding can only occur with sexually mature animals. Most captive-bred kingsnakes must be at least two years old in order to successfully breed. If you

California kingsnakes *(Lampropeltis getula californiae)* breeding. Photo by Glen Carlzen.

An albino California kingsnake *(Lampropeltis getula californiae)* laying eggs. It is recommended that an egg-laying container with a moist substratum be provided for females ready to lay eggs. Photo by Robert Applegate.

A California kingsnake *(Lampropeltis getula californiae)* hatching. These are among the easiest snakes to breed in captivity and are highly recommended for beginners. Photo by Glen Carlzen.

Kingsnake *(Lampropeltis getula)* eggs can be readily incubated in plastic shoeboxes containing moistened vermiculite. Photo by Glen Carlzen.

cannot assess the age of your snakes, size is a good criterion for determining sexual maturity. Most sexually mature common kingsnakes are at least thirty-six inches long (they may breed at a smaller size but this is the minimum criterion used by most breeders). The rule of thumb for kingsnakes used to be eighteen months until sexual maturity if maintained on an optimal growth feeding schedule. Many breeders, however, prefer to wait an extra year to allow for extra growth before breeding. Breeding at an early age or minimal size can result in stunting that will ultimately affect the breeding ability of an animal. The chances for an animal becoming egg-bound also increase. Breeders have found it a better strategy to allow a more normal growth pattern and wait until their animals are at least two years old (usually two and a half) before attempting breeding.

The other important consideration before conditioning your kingsnakes for breeding will be their health status. An animal that is not in prime condition should never be considered for breeding. Not only will the chances for successful breeding diminish, the actual gestation period may be life threatening. The chances of the female becoming eggbound will also significantly increase if she is ill, underweight or undersized.

BREEDING FORMULA
Although there are many subspecies of kingsnakes inhabiting diverse terrain, altitude, climatic zones, etc., general parameters for successful breeding can be applied to all subspecies. These include proper feeding regimen, pre-breeding conditioning which may involve cooling, the actual introduction of animals for breeding, monitoring of the females, providing egglaying sites, and proper egg incubation.

PROPER FEEDING SCHEDULES
Refer to Feeding under Feeding Regimens for Breeding Kingsnakes.

PRE-BREEDING CONDITIONING
The standard procedure for pre-breeding conditioning of kingsnakes involves cooling them for at least two months at a specific, constant

lowered temperature range. All the subspecies of kingsnakes may be conditioned for breeding by using this procedure. It is important to note that snakes do not hibernate in the technically literal sense of the word during the winter months. Hibernation implies a state of dormancy wherein an animal is inactive. The scant research that has been done on reptile behavior suggests that they will emerge from their winter shelters during days that are abnormally warm. This type of wintering behavior, in which there may be continual albeit reduced activity, is called "brumation." Most herpetoculturists, however, continue to use the term "hibernation" when referring to the cooling process and the reduced activity associated with it. Because the meaning of hibernation in a herpetocultural sense is generally understood, the author will continue to use hibernation and hibernate in the rest of the text. Because of this activity during hibernation, fresh water should always be provided during the cooling period. Care must be given to provide water in topple-proof containers that are only half filled, to eliminate the possibility of water spillage.

As a general rule, kingsnakes should be cooled to between 50 and 60°F for a period of eight to twelve weeks. Most kingsnakes, however, will safely tolerate temperature drops into the upper 40's°F. During this time, lights should be turned off or the photoperiod significantly reduced. Some kingsnake breeders pay careful attention to the photoperiod (amount of daylight compared to darkness) during this time, and suggest that it is at least as important as cooling. Other successful breeders simply keep their animals in dark areas during the entire cooling period. Basically, the photoperiod is reduced to ten hours or even less for the winter months.

During hibernation, it is important to regularly check snakes for any kind of diseases, especially respiratory infections. If the setup is allowed to become wet, skin blisters are another disease which can occur at this time. If there is a problem, the snake should be removed from hibernation immediately and treated accordingly. The probability of any of these happening will be significantly reduced if the snakes are in top condition prior to the cooling period. If you have any doubts about a snake's health, that particular animal simply should not be hibernated.

"Banana" morph of the California kingsnake (*Lampropeltis getula californiae*), sometimes sold as 75% yellow or 90% yellow California kingsnakes. They are the result of selective breeding originating from a cross between a Newport striped phase and an odd chain patterned California kingsnake. This strain was established by Frank Retes, one of the pioneers in the development of kingsnake herpetoculture. Photo by Glen Carlzen.

SAMPLE KINGSNAKE BREEDING OUTCOMES (opposite page) In the upper example, a normal AA California kingsnake is crossed with an amelanistic albino specimen aa. The normal gene A, which will result in the presence of black pigmentation, is dominant over the recessive albino gene a. When the normal specimen AA is crossed with the albino aa, as demonstrated by the Punnett square, all offspring will appear normal because A is dominant over a. However, they will all be heterozygous for albinism and carry the albino a gene. Thus, all will be Aa.

In the lower example, two heterozygous for albinism Aa, are bred together. Using a Punnett square, we find that there will be a 25% probability of homozygous normal-colored AA, a 50% probability of normal-appearing heterozygous for albinism Aa, and a 25% probability of albino aa specimens.

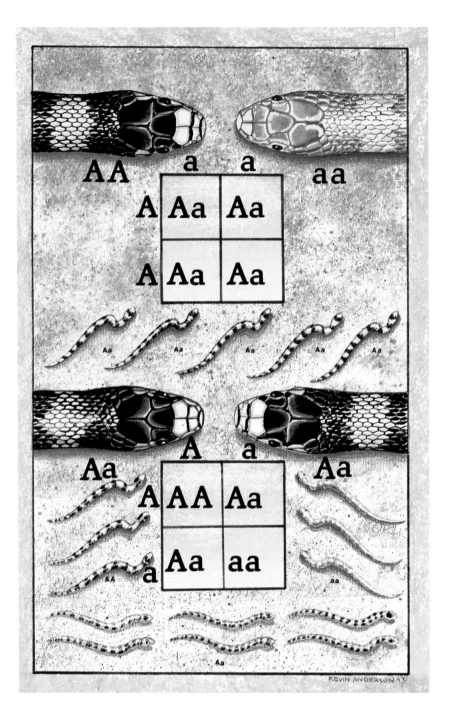

These pre-breeding procedures are necessary for consistent breeding success and high fertility rates. The dormant period in cool conditions is believed to cause female kingsnakes to produce hormones which stimulate ovulation, and pheromones (sex hormones) which elicit sexual behavior in males. The cool period for males triggers an increase in male hormone levels which elicits mating behavior and the production of healthy, active sperm.

BREEDING

When the kingsnakes are first removed from being cooled, their health should be checked right away. If there are health problems, they should be attended to immediately, so that perhaps the affected animal(s) can still be bred.

If the snakes are healthy coming out of hibernation, then conditioning for breeding can commence right away. Warming the animals to normal maintenance temperatures, and providing an extended photoperiod, are the first steps. However, many commercial breeders will pay no attention to the photoperiod; kingsnakes will breed readily in low light conditions. They should be tried on food within two to three days after return to normal maintenance temperatures. It can sometimes take a week to ten days before kingsnakes out of hibernation start feeding. A snake that is reluctant to start feeding might be tried with a smaller-than-normal rodent. Offer food frequently until an animal starts feeding. When kingsnakes start feeding after hibernation, they usually do it with gusto. As during normal maintenance procedures, animals should always be separated during feeding. The feeding period from the time that kingsnakes are taken out of hibernation until sexual pairs are introduced for breeding can be critical, especially for somewhat underweight animals. In females, intensive feeding during this period can play a crucial role in their fecundity for a given year.

As a start, right after hibernation, one or two rodents of appropriate size should be given to each snake every two to three days. Two to four large mice or fuzzy rats can be fed to very large specimens, such as *L. g. getula*, every two to three days. Kingsnakes will usually be able to handle this amount of food. Some might want more, some less, or they might not want to eat quite that often. In any event, the feeding pattern should be established within the first week and adhered to throughout this phase of conditioning.

The length of time this accelerated feeding schedule lasts will be determined to a significant degree by how soon the snake will be ready to breed. A primary purpose of accelerated feeding is to put weight on snakes that are slightly underweight after removal from hibernation. Usually a three to six week period is sufficient to prime both sexes for breeding. Since snakes lose very little weight during hibernation, a snake coming out of hibernation that is thin probably went into hibernation being thin. A snake that is obviously under-weight should not be hibernated.

Following removal from hibernation, the first shed (possibly second shed if a female is undergoing a shed cycle upon removal from hibernation) of a female kingsnake is usually associated with ovula-tion and the production of pheromones. It is generally recommended that you should begin introduction of pairs following the first shed after removal from hibernation. Many breeders will start introduc-tions earlier. In the case of speckled kingsnakes which breed soon after removal from hibernation, pairs are introduced for short periods of time starting one week after their return to normal maintenance schedules. There is a critical breeding window (the onset of which is usually associated with the first shed following removal from hibernation) and waiting too long may cause the animals to be out of breeding synchronization which could result in little or no breeding success. One way to be certain a female is ready to breed is to feel for developing ovarian egg follicles. This procedure is referred to as palpation. Palpating a female kingsnake involves gently pushing in the ventral scales toward the backbone, starting at about mid-body and continuing toward the vent. The follicles feel like a series of bumps and one can even go so far as determining the number of eggs that will be laid. If you can feel the follicles, then your snake is ready to breed and a male should be introduced. Gentle palpation is the key to determining if follicles have formed.

VARIATION IN THE BLOTCHED KINGSNAKE
(Lampropeltis getula "goini")

An adult blotched specimen. Photo by Bill Love.

An evenly speckled specimen. Photo by Bill Love.

A specimen with faint mid-dorsal striping. Photo by Bill Love.

Copulation usually occurs immediately following introduction, with the male chasing the female around the cage until she is caught. The male will normally grab the female with his mouth, holding her behind the head, and positioning his body until their vents meet, one of the male's hemipenes enters the female's cloaca, and copulation occurs. This will last anywhere from several minutes to several hours. If successive breedings occur, the male will alternate hemipenes each time. The snakes can be kept together for two to three days until they must be fed. They should then be separated so that they can be fed safely and to allow the male to regenerate sperm for the next breeding. They should be reintroduced several times over the next three to four weeks to insure high fertility. If there are several pairs involved, then it may be wise to introduce the females to more than one male unless one is involved in careful line breeding that requires that exact records are maintained as to the father of a particular group of offspring. Using more than one male is a precaution in case one of the males is infertile. Keeping careful breeding records will, however, allow you to determine males who tend to "perform" consistently. A "dud" male may copulate without releasing viable sperm because of one or more factors that have led to sterility. Any successful breeding program should involve more than one pair of animals to minimize the possiblity of a sterile male. A useful method for determining the fertility of males and probable successful copulation is to obtain a cloacal smear onto a microscope slide from a recently copulated female. The smear can then be examined under a microscope at a low magnification, to check for the presence of active spermatozoa.

After you are certain that the snakes have bred, then separate the female(s) from the male(s). A gravid female snake will demonstrate significant abdominal swelling that can usually be easily seen or that can be readily palpated. A gravid female will usually also become more reluctant to feed on large prey and may go off feed completely as gestation progresses. A good indication that the female is about to lay eggs is the pre-egglaying shed (usually the second shed after removal from hibernation). This usually occurs five to ten days before the eggs are laid. Feeding schedules, as discussed earlier, should be followed and a nest box should be put into the female's cage. This box should be large enough so that the snake can get in and lay her eggs. The author has used a two quart plastic storage container containing moistened vermiculite. A small hole should be cut in the lid for entry. The timing of putting the nest box in the cage is a matter of choice, although it should be no later than the pre-egglaying shed. The time between copulation and egg deposition in kingsnakes usually ranges from six to twelve weeks.

After breeding and separating the snakes, female kingsnakes may go off feed as gestation progresses. Gravid females should be offered small prey animals, such as fuzzy mice, if they refuse larger adult mice. It is not uncommon for females to go off feed or refuse larger prey during this time. This should not be a problem if a female has good weight.

INCUBATING THE EGGS
Once the eggs have been deposited, hopefully in the nest box, they should be set up in an appropriate incubator. This should not be too complex, as they should be kept at the same temperature as your snakes, simply with higher humidity. This can be accomplished by burying the eggs halfway in moist vermiculite (equal parts of vermiculite and water by weight) in a plastic shoe box with a few small holes for air exchange, which is very important for developing embryos. Most of the time eggs are deposited in a clump with the shells adhering to each other. They should not be separated or you risk damaging the eggs. The author has successfully hatched many clutches of eggs that were clumped together. Sometimes one or more infertile eggs may be included in a clump of good eggs. The bad eggs will become obvious after a few weeks of incubation. Don't try to remove them from the rest. The author has successfully hatched many clutches of eggs in this same condition.

Eggs should be incubated at a constant temperature of 82-84°F in a coarse grade of vermiculite which has been mixed with an equal amount of water by weight. The vermiculite should feel barely moist and not waterlogged. An easy method of incubation is to use an aquarium with a few inches of water on the bottom which is heated by a submersible aquarium heater. The temperature should be adjusted with the aid of a thermometer, allowing several days of lead time before eggs are introduced. As stated earlier, a plastic storage box is suitable for incubating eggs. The shoe box, with moistened vermiculite, is placed on bricks or a sturdy wire rack above the water and allowed to heat up to the ambient air temperature within the aquarium. The humidity is regulated by partially covering the top of the aquarium. The eggs should be placed in the incubator when the temperature of the vermiculite in the incubator box has stabilized to 82-84°F for at least 48 hours.

The babies should hatch in eight to ten weeks. Like most snakes, kingsnakes will not emerge immediately after slitting their shells. It is very important not to attempt to help them hatch. Only twenty-four hours after the snake has first poked its head out should providing help be considered. There are those occasions when the baby, with its egg tooth cutting its way out, will shred the shell and become stuck between shell sections. When this happens, use cuticle scissors to make 90 degree incisions through the slits made by the hatching snake. Snakes that have failed to slit their shells within 36 hours of the rest of the clutch, should be assisted by making a 1 inch by 1/4 inch incision at the high point of the top side of the egg. These incisions are made so that only the shell is pierced, making sure the scissors do not penetrate any deeper.

Hatchling kingsnakes need to be maintained separately in individual enclosures. This will allow for close monitoring of each animal and will allow you to determine such things as when a snake first sheds, how well it feeds, and whether it will need any special attention. Caging animals individually will also prevent the possibility of cannibalism from occurring during feeding. Please refer to the section entitled Feeding if necessary.

DOUBLE CLUTCHING

There are several factors which can influence the production of a second clutch of eggs.

1) Age and size. It is best to attempt double clutching with older, larger females.

2) Health and relative weight. It is very important to observe the condition of the female after laying her first clutch. She must be in good health, not too thin or lethargic.

3) Timing of the introduction of a male followed by an appropriate feeding regimen. If the female appears relatively robust, then proceed to introduce her to a male soon after she has laid her eggs. Don't assume copulation will occur, because timing is everything. It has been reported that if this second introduction occurs too late in the year, the female won't be interested in breeding. If copulation is observed, then you must assume she has been impregnated and proceed with an accelerated feeding schedule once again. This involves feeding 2-3 adult mice or fuzzy rats every three to four days. Again, it is probable that the female will become a reluctant feeder during gestation and should be offered smaller food items to try to get her to feed. For double clutching, feeding during the first clutching is essential (see Feeding Adults section).

Notes on Breeding the Various Subspecies

BLOTCHED KINGSNAKE (*Lampropeltis getula "goini"*) AND
SOUTH FLORIDA KINGSNAKE (*Lampropeltis getula "brooksi"*)
Minimum breeding age: 2 to 3 years.
When Cooled: Start cooling in December to the beginning of March. However, these subspecies can be cooled for only two months with good breeding success.
Temperature for cooling: Mid 50's (°F).
When sexual pairs are put together: Sexual pairs are introduced mid-March, although the vast majority of breeding takes place in April.
When eggs are laid: Six to eight weeks after breeding. Most eggs are laid in June, although they can lay first clutches as early as May.
Clutch size: Ten to twenty eggs are laid per clutch, with sixteen to seventeen as average.
Number of clutches: Both subspecies will double clutch if properly maintained and conditioned for breeding, especially "*goini.*"
Breeding difficulties with phenotypic or geographical variants: None.

CALIFORNIA, DESERT, MEXICAN BLACK AND YUMA KINGSNAKES, (*L. g. californiae, splendida, nigrita, and "yumensis"*)
Minimum breeding age: 2 to 3 years.
When cooled: Start cooling in December to beginning of March.
Temperature for cooling: Low to mid 50's (°F).
When sexual pairs are put together: All four forms breed six weeks after hibernation.
When eggs are laid: Six to eight weeks after breeding.
Clutch size: California king-6 to 23 for coastal types, 6 to 12 for desert phase; Desert king-6 to 12; Yuma king-6 to 12; Mexican Black king-6 to 20.

SPECKLED KINGSNAKE (*Lampropeltis getula holbrooki*)
Minimum breeding age: 2 to 3 years.
When Cooled: December 1 to March 1.
Temperature for cooling: Low to mid 50's (°F).
When sexual pairs are introduced: This subspecies is atypical in that pairs should be introduced no later than two weeks after removal from hibernation and will even breed as early as one week after removal.
When eggs are laid: Six to eight weeks after breeding.
Clutch size: Six to twenty-two eggs.
Number of clutches: Will double clutch if female is on the large size. Smaller animals simply don't double clutch.
Breeding difficulties: None, except for early introduction of pairs.

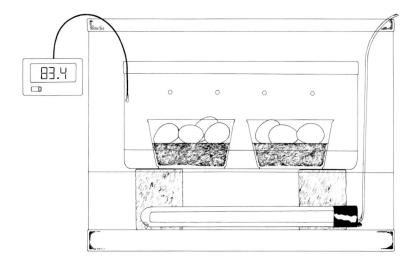

Front view of an incubator using an aquarium and a submersible heater. The eggs are placed in containers inside a storage box on two bricks. Enough water is added to cover the submersible heater which is then adjusted with the aid of a thermometer. The top of the aquarium is then covered leaving a small space for airflow.

Source Materials

Conant, R. 1975. *A Field Guide to Reptiles and Amphibians of Eastern and Central North America.* Houghton Mifflin Co., Boston.

Frost, D.R. and J.T. Collins. 1988. Nomenclatural notes on reptiles of the United States. *Herpetological Review*, 19(4): 73-76.

Frye, F. 1991. *Reptile Care Vols. 1 & 2.* TFH Pub.

Markell, R. 1990. *Kingsnakes and Milksnakes.* TFH Pub.

Mattison, C. 1988. *Keeping and Breeding Snakes.* Blandford Press, London.

Mills, T. "To Scent or Not to Scent." *The Vivarium.* 1989, 2(3): 8-10, 27.

Stebbins, R. 1966. *A Field Guide to Western Reptiles and Amphibians.*

Wright, A.H. and A.A. Wright. 1957. *Handbook of Snakes of the United States and Canada.* Comstock Publ. Co., New York.

DISTRIBUTION OF *LAMPROPELTIS GETULA* SUBSPECIES
AND VARIANTS RECOGNIZED BY HERPETOCULTURISTS

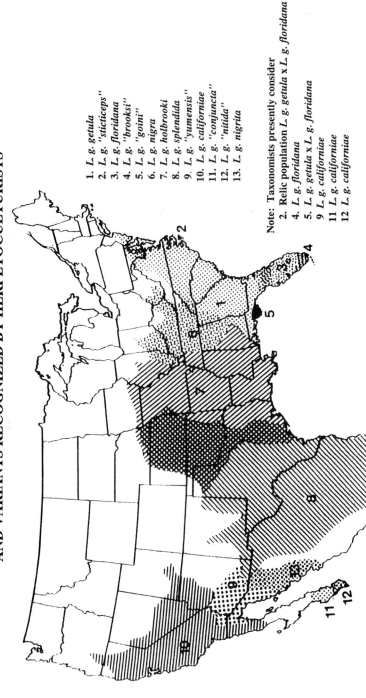

1. *L. g. getula*
2. *L. g. "sticticeps"*
3. *L. g. floridana*
4. *L. g. "brooksi"*
5. *L. g. "goini"*
6. *L. g. nigra*
7. *L. g. holbrooki*
8. *L. g. splendida*
9. *L. g. "yumensis"*
10. *L. g. californiae*
11. *L. g. "conjuncta"*
12. *L. g. "nitida"*
13. *L. g. nigrita*

Note: Taxonomists presently consider

2. Relic population *L. g. getula* x *L. g. floridana*
4. *L. g. floridana*
5. *L. g. getula* x *L. g. floridana*
9 *L. g. californiae*
11 *L. g. californiae*
12 *L. g. californiae*